I0794837

# The Zoo

by Giulia Verzariu
illustrated by Diane Paterson

Pre-Decodable 7

McGraw Hill Education

*Bothell, WA • Chicago, IL • Columbus, OH • New York, NY*

**MHEonline.com**

Copyright © 2015 McGraw-Hill Education

All rights reserved. No part of this publication may be reproduced or distributed in any form or by any means, or stored in a database or retrieval system, without the prior written consent of McGraw-Hill Education, including, but not limited to, network storage or transmission, or broadcast for distance learning.

Send all inquiries to:
McGraw-Hill Education
8787 Orion Place
Columbus, OH 43240

ISBN: 978-0-02-145194-4
MHID: 0-02-145194-X

Printed in China

9 10 11 12 13 DSS 28 27 26 25 24

The  had .

zoo

animals

The  had .

zebra stripes

The  had 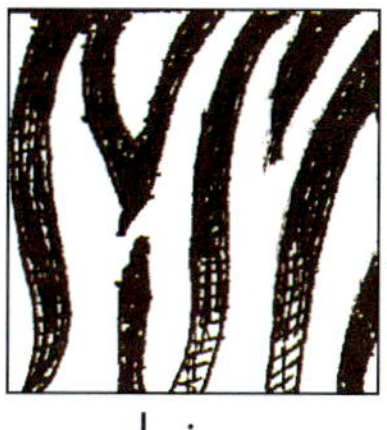.

tiger stripes

The  had 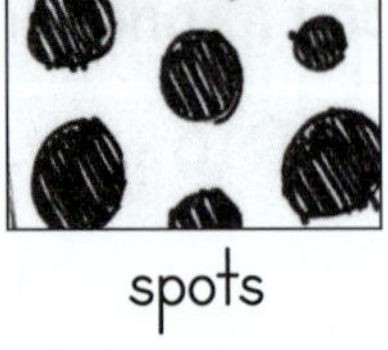.

giraffe spots

The  had .

owl spots

The  had 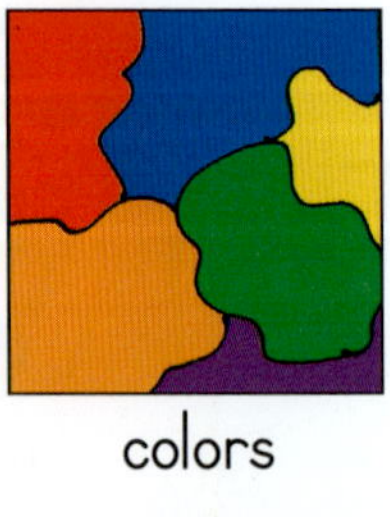 !

peacock colors